# pop zone TEEN QUEENS

BY MONICA RIZZO

Scholastic Inc.

New York   Toronto   London   Auckland   Sydney
Mexico City   New Delhi   Hong Kong   Buenos Aires

Photo Credits:

Cover: (top left) Russell Boyce: Reuters NewMedia Inc./CORBIS; (top right) Stewart Volland/Retna Ltd.; (bottom left) Stewart Volland/Retna Ltd.; (bottom right) Luis Martinez/AFF/Retna Ltd.
Page 3: Everett Collection; Page 4: Jean-Paul Aussenard/WireImage.com; Page 5: Jim Spellman/WireImage.com; Page 6: Liam Duke/Camera Press/Retna Ltd.; Page 7: (left) Bill Davila/Retna Ltd., (right) Darla Khazei/Retna Ltd.; Page 8: Everett Collection; Page 9: (left) Arun Nevader/WireImage.com, (right) Tammie Arroyo/Retna Ltd.; Page 10: Everett Collection; Page 11: Stewart Volland/Retna Ltd.; Page 12: Stewart Volland/Retna Ltd.; Page 13: Everett Collection; Page 14: Walter McBride/Retna Ltd.; Page 15: Everett Collection; Page 16: John Spellman/Retna Ltd.; Page 17: Everett Collection; Page 18: Everett Collection; Page 19: Sara De Boer/Retna Ltd.; Page 20: Paul Smith/Feature Flash/Retna Ltd.; Page 21: Everett Collection; Page 22: Jeff Slocomb/Retna Ltd.; Page 23: Jeff Slocomb/Retna Ltd.; Page 24: Sara De Boer/Retna Ltd.; Page 25: Stewart Volland/Retna Ltd.; Page 26: Everett Collection; Page 27: Michelle Roberts/Retna Ltd.; Page 28: Everett Collection; Page 29: Jean-Paul Aussenard/WireImage.com; Page 30: Jean-Paul Aussenard/WireImage.com; Page 31: Sara De Boer/Retna Ltd.

Photo Editor: Sharon Lennon

ISBN 0-439-62336-7

Design by Madalina Stefan Blanton

Printed in the U.S.A.

First printing, November 2003

Teen queen Alexis Bledel with her onscreen mom Lauren Graham.

**H**as there been a time in Hollywood when so many girls ruled television, movies, *and* music? These days you have to have more than one talent to succeed, and this crop of Teen Queens is off-the-hook hot!

Mandy, Hilary, and Solange juggle music and movie careers. Gals like Alexis, Mary-Kate and Ashley, Amanda, and Raven do films and television.

On the verge of greatness are Kristin, Brittany, and a slew of "fresh faces" like Kaley, Alexa, Jennifer, and Emily.

They're all wonderful performers — and that's because they love what they do. Ask any one of them how they do it all, and they will tell you that they're just like you. Read on to learn more about your favorite stars. You might be surprised to see just how much *you* have in common with these incredible young women.

# Alexis Bledel
## (Gilmore Girls)

As straight-A student and all-around-good-person Rory Gilmore, Alexis Bledel makes life look easy. She handles school, friends, dating, her mom, and her grandparents simply and directly. How does she do it? Alexis says it's just luck. "I didn't know anything going into it," she says when she heard she got the part on the hit WB series *Gilmore Girls*. Acting, she says, comes "naturally."

Whatever the case, Alexis is certainly one of the most watchable and likable gals around. Much like Rory, she loves to read and is totally into school. In fact, she was a freshman at New York University when she got the *Gilmore Girls* gig. "I'd love to go back [to col-

| | |
|---|---|
| **BIRTHDATE**: | September 16, 1981 |
| **ASTRO SIGN**: | Virgo |
| **HOMETOWN**: | Houston, Texas |
| **BIG BREAK**: | The hit TV show *Gilmore Girls* |
| **WHAT'S NEXT**: | Independent film *The Orphan King*, returning to New York University some day to finish earning a degree in film |
| **FAVORITE LIP GLOSS**: | Tarte lipstick |
| **FAVE MUSICAL ACTS**: | Less Than Jake, Everclear |
| **ACTING ROLE MODELS**: | Emily Watson, Samantha Morton, Robin Wright Penn |
| **LIKES TO EAT**: | Macaroni and cheese |
| **HOBBIES**: | Music, hiking, reading, shopping at Target |
| **SHE ADMIRES**: | Her parents. "They've been supportive of me my whole life." |

lege]," she says. But for now the show is an education for Alexis. "Rory is evolving and so am I," says Alexis, who relates to Rory because "she's an intelligent character whose goals aren't like those of other people her age."

Los Angeles is a long way from Alexis's hometown of Houston, Texas, where she took acting classes as a kid to overcome her shyness. Being onstage allowed her to express herself and discover that "most actors are shy. They're reserved, private people who use acting as an outlet for expressing themselves."

At fourteen Alexis signed up with a local modeling agency that got her plenty of work in print ads for department stores and fashion shoots for *Seventeen* magazine. "Modeling can be great," Alexis says. "I got to travel and meet people." She continued to model until she enrolled at NYU "to be a filmmaker and write and direct my own features," she explains.

Last summer Alexis stayed west so she could star in the movie *Tuck Everlasting* with too-cute-to-be-for-real Jonathan Jackson. Of course Alexis aced the movie and won rave reviews. She shuns the praise. "I think I'm very professionally lucky. I've been at the right places at the right time," she says.

One place you'll probably never see Alexis is Starbucks. Why? She hates coffee. Rory downs plenty at Luke's Diner, but that's because Alexis fills her mug with cola! Her favorite real-life hangout is Target. "When I am bored I go to Target. When I am upset I go to Target. My best friend and I both really like going to Target," Alexis says, laughing.

Unlike other actors who stress and obsess about their next job, Alexis is just going to go with the flow. "I just picture myself being happy," she says. "You've just got to make your plans and once you've made them you have to stop worrying."

Alexis Bledel gets all glammed up with co-star Milo Ventimiglia.

**FILL-IN FAVES:**

On *Gilmore Girls*, Rory hangs out at Luke's Diner. When I'm hanging with my friends I like to go to <u>the mall</u>
because <u>It's fun to shop</u>
Alexis loves to read. My favorite book to read is <u>Freaky Friday</u>
because <u>I saw the movie and I liked it</u>.
If I could go to any concert with Alexis, who loves music, I would take her to see <u>Avril Lavigne</u>
because <u>She rocks</u>!

# MandyMoore

## MORE ABOUT MANDY

**F**our years ago Mandy Moore was "just another blond singer" in the crazy pop music world, trying to make a name for herself while facing stiff competition from Britney Spears and Christina Aguilera. But it didn't take long for Mandy to prove that she was more than a pretty face. Critics and fans both agreed that Mandy was a unique talent with her smash debut CD *So Real*. Proving she was the real deal, Mandy followed up with three more bestselling CDs, her own MTV show, and a lead role opposite hunky Shane West in the movie *A Walk to Remember*.

Now nineteen, Mandy stands head and shoulders above the crowd (literally — she's 5' 10" tall!) in terms of talent and versatility. This fall she will release her fifth CD, *Coverage*, and will star in two feature films — *How To Deal* and *Saved*.

| | |
|---|---|
| **BIRTHDATE:** | April 10, 1984 |
| **ASTRO SIGN:** | Aries |
| **HOMETOWN:** | Orlando, Florida |
| **BIG BREAK:** | Singing the national anthem at an Orlando Magic basketball game |
| **WHAT'S NEXT:** | Feature films *How To Deal, Saved,* and *First Daughter*. A new CD, *Coverage,* is due out in fall 2003 |
| **FAVORITE ENTERTAINER:** | Bette Midler |
| **FAVORITE FOOD:** | Sushi |
| **PETS:** | Two Yorkshire Terriers Winston and Oliver. Three cats Milo, Chloe, and Zoe |
| **LIKES TO READ:** | Magazines. "I'm a magazine-a-holic!" Mandy declares. |
| **HOBBIES:** | Reading (see above), getting manicures, listening to music |

Mandy hasn't missed a step since debuting as a singer in her hometown of Orlando, Florida. As a young girl, her voice captured everyone's attention. Mandy soon became known as "the National Anthem girl" because she was regularly booked for Orlando Magic basketball games and other sporting events in town. Soon she was tapped for local commercials, radio jingles, and voiceover work. When Mandy was thirteen, a FedEx deliveryman heard her singing in an Orlando studio. He liked what he heard so much that he referred her to a top-notch music executive who wasted no time offering Mandy a deal.

Two years later, Mandy became a massive success. "This whole last four-year period has been a dream and I just don't want to wake up. I have come to love acting but will never give up on the singing career," Mandy says.

Right now Mandy is happy — and busy — doing both. And she's even found time to date hunky pro tennis player Andy Roddick. Dating an athlete has been a learning experience for Mandy. "I knew nothing about tennis until I met him," she confesses. "Now I'm so into it."

She's also into shopping (what gal isn't?), music, and acting. But if it were all to end tomorrow, Mandy wouldn't freak. She'd probably go to college and "study to be a journalist." No matter what happens, she says, "I'd like to be remembered as someone who is true. A good friend. Honest. And someone who doesn't live with boundaries. Someone who reaches beyond people's expectations."

"I'm so geeky! I'm very silly and I trip a lot." —Mandy

FILL-IN FAVES:

Mandy says she's a klutzy geek. The most embarrassing thing that ever happened to me is _____.

When I want some time to myself, I _____.

Tennis has become a favorite sport of Mandy's. My favorite athletic outing is _____ because _____.

# Raven

| | |
|---|---|
| **BIRTHDATE**: | December 10, 1985 |
| **ASTRO SIGN**: | Sagittarius |
| **HOMETOWN**: | Atlanta, Georgia |
| **BIG BREAK**: | Starring on *The Cosby Show* when she was three years old |
| **WHAT'S NEXT**: | Continuing with *That's So Raven* on the Disney Channel; the movie *Cheetah Girls* for the Disney Channel with singing group 3LW |
| **FAVORITE LIP GLOSS**: | MAC Lip Glass |
| **NICKNAME**: | Rae |
| **PET PEEVE**: | Fake people |
| **ROLE MODEL**: | Bill Cosby |
| **HOBBIES**: | Shopping, music, getting manicures |

A young Raven on *The Cosby Show*.

Turn on the tube and you'll likely see Raven all over. You can catch her on *That's So Raven*, her Disney Channel show about a psychic teenager. Click around on the remote and you might also catch Raven in reruns of *The Cosby Show* or *Hangin' With Mr. Cooper*.

Yes, Raven is just about everywhere these days — and she couldn't be happier. She's having a lot of fun and it shows in her work. Raven says, "It's really not a challenge for me to be funny all the time. That's how I like to be normally."

She was born on December 10, 1985, and named Raven-Symone Christina Pearman in Atlanta, Georgia. Once she started modeling, at the age of three, she went by her first name, Raven-Symone. Her family moved to New York in 1989 and young Raven-Symone was signed by the prestigious Ford Modeling Agency. She was sent out on numerous auditions, including one for the movie *Ghost Dad*, which starred Bill Cosby. Well, it turned out she was a little too young for the role. But Mr. Cosby, as she calls him, thought she showed great promise. So he asked her to join the cast of his hit television show, *The Cosby Show*. Of course, she said yes — and ended up playing his granddaughter, Olivia Kendall, for three seasons. What was it like working with a comedy legend? "His advice has gotten me this far," she explains. "Stay professional and always stay sweet." And, she says, "Have fun when you do your work."

The show ended in 1992, but Raven's career was just warming up. She immediately landed another television series, *Hangin' With Mr. Cooper*, and had a role in the movie *The Little Rascals*. But wait, that's not all. She could also sing like an angel and at age five Raven had signed a recording deal with MCA records. She released a CD called *Unforgettable* and even toured with 'N Sync! Talk about busy!

In 2001, the Disney Channel snapped her up to star in her own show, *That's So Raven* (she also sings the show's theme song). She decided to drop "Symone" because, "I'm getting older and it's a lot easier for me, a lot more personal and makes the public feel closer," she explains.

Raven, a high school senior, studies as

much as she can while she's working. "School is important to me — I want to go to college." Keeping on top of it all is a real challenge, Raven says. "With this show, one minute I'm on the set, one minute I'm studying the War of 1812." Yup, that's so Raven.

## FILL-IN FAVES:

Raven's role model is comedian Bill Cosby. My role model is _____ because _____.

Raven has the ability to see into the future on her show, *That's So Raven*. If I could have one secret power it would be _____ because _____.

Nicknames are cool. I like when people call me ___Sydster___ instead of my first name.

# AmandaBynes

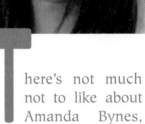

| | |
|---|---|
| BIRTHDATE: | April 3, 1986 |
| ASTRO SIGN: | Aries |
| HOMETOWN: | Thousand Oaks, California |
| BIG BREAK: | Appearing in *All That* on Nickelodeon when she was ten |
| WHAT'S NEXT: | The second season of *What I Like About You* on the W.B. Amanda also lends her voice to the animated movie *Robots*, due in 2005 |

| FAVORITE | |
|---|---|
| LIP GLOSS: | Prescriptives |
| SNACKS ON: | Red Hots and plain M&M's |
| FAVE MEAL: | Breakfast. Amanda loves chocolate-chip pancakes |
| SHE WATCHES: | *Friends, The Simpsons, Felicity* |
| PETS: | Tootsie, a golden Lab, and Betty, an Australian shepherd |
| FAVE BOOK: | *Matilda*, by Roald Dahl |
| HOBBIES: | Shopping, music, sleeping in, going to amusement parks |

here's not much not to like about Amanda Bynes, star of the WB comedy *What I Like About You* and the hit movies *Big Fat Liar* (with *Malcolm in the Middle*'s Frankie Muniz) and *What a Girl Wants*. She's cute, she's cheerful, and she's very, very funny. In fact, Amanda can't remember a time she didn't like to make people laugh. "I was always kind of goofy," Amanda says. "And I had all this energy."

Like a lot of kids, Amanda loved going to camp every summer. One year her dad surprised her with a different kind of activity — a summer comedy camp at a Los Angeles club called the Laugh Factory. The never-shy Amanda quickly learned the ropes of improvisational and sketch comedy. So fast, in fact, the producers of the hot Nickelodeon show *All That* signed Amanda to a contract when she was only ten years old! She immediately fit in with the show's stars Kenan Thompson and Kel Mitchell. "Getting to put on wigs and props and doing characters was perfect for me," Amanda says.

Amanda developed funny impersonations of newswoman Barbara Walters and TV personality Judge Judy. It wasn't long before she had blossomed into a full-fledged superstar and was hosting her own Nickelodeon variety series, *The Amanda Show*. She was a huge hit. Critics started comparing her to comedy legend Lucille Ball — something Amanda considers a huge compliment.

"Whenever I was sad or whenever I was feeling down, I would always watch an episode [of the *I Love Lucy* show], and she would make me laugh. She's a very talented person," Amanda says.

That's typical Amanda. She may be a star in other people's eyes, but in real life she's just a down-to-earth teenager who's also a fan of other actors. While Amanda was jazzed about her big-screen debut with Frankie Muniz in *Big Fat Liar*, it was her second movie that gave her the jitters. When Amanda heard that British actor Colin Firth was going to star as her dad in *What a Girl Wants*, she freaked. "I wanted to work with him so badly and I was shocked that he would even be near me, let alone do a movie with me," Amanda says.

The movie was filmed in London, England, where he's a big star. So it's no wonder Amanda was totally surprised when people recognized her. "While we were doing a scene on the Millennium Bridge in London, a student outing of about five hundred kids happened to walk past. Some kid recognized me and started shouting my name, 'Amanda!' Then the rest of them started doing it, too. It was pretty overwhelming trying to do this scene when I'm hearing all these people screaming 'Amanda!'"

Amanda loves her fans, but swears she doesn't get the hype. "I don't live my life in the actress-y kind of way. I like doing what I do, becoming another person and doing roles, so being famous kind of comes along with it." She adds, "I am the same as any girl." And *that's* what we like most about Amanda.

About *All That*: "Getting to put on wigs and props and doing characters was perfect for me."

Amanda likes going to amusement parks. My favorite ride in an amusement park is _____ because _____

Birthdays are cool. Amanda recently had a birthday cake with her picture on it. The best birthday I ever had was when I turned _____ because _____

*What a Girl Wants* was filmed in

     a)  New Orleans.

     b)  McDonald's.

     c)  London.

     d)  my backyard.

# Brittany Snow

| | |
|---|---|
| **BIRTHDATE:** | March 9, 1986 |
| **ASTRO SIGN:** | Pisces |
| **HOMETOWN:** | Tampa, Florida |
| **BIG BREAK:** | Playing bad girl Susan Lemay for two seasons on the soap opera *Guiding Light* |
| **WHAT'S NEXT:** | The second season of the NBC drama *American Dreams*, and graduating high school |
| **FAVORITE ICE CREAM:** | Cookies and cream or cookie dough |
| **FAVORITE SCHOOL SUBJECT:** | English ("I hate math," Brittany declares) |
| **HOBBIES:** | Listening to music, talking on the phone with her friends, reading, going to the movies |
| **RECENTLY READ:** | *Chicken Soup for the Teenage Soul* |
| **WHAT SHE WATCHES:** | *Friends, Buffy the Vampire Slayer* |
| **FAVORITE ACTRESS:** | Meg Ryan |

**B**rittany Snow has a dream job these days as Meg Pryor, a sweet and passionate teenager on the NBC family drama *American Dreams*, which is set in the 1960s. It's a time when the world was experiencing tremendous changes in politics (Martin Luther King Jr. and John F. Kennedy) and music (the Beatles).

"The show is like a huge history lesson for me. I love going to work every day," says Brittany, who started modeling in her hometown of Tampa, Florida, when she was three years old. When she was five, she would have her friends over and direct them in backyard plays (she was the star, of course). "If they didn't get their lines right, I would yell at them: 'It's not just a line — this is serious!'" Brittany says.

A year later, Brittany was cast in several local commercials. When she was twelve, she got her big break playing bratty teenager Susan Lemay for three years on the soap opera *Guiding Light*, which tapes in New York. "I was always the nice girl next door. I loved playing bad," Brittany confesses.

Still, life away from home was difficult. "There was no tutor on the set in New York, so I would have to teach myself," explains Brittany, a straight-A student. "Then my mother and I would fly home and I would go to school to take my tests and get my assignments for the next week. Then we would fly back and I had to memorize thirty to forty pages of lines."

Brittany took a one-year break from the mega-grueling schedule so she could "do the normal high school things" like go to dances and shop with her friends.

When she was offered the part on *American Dreams*, Brittany couldn't say no. "It took my breath away," says Brittany, who is also hooked on sixties music.

*American Dreams* features current artists who perform songs from the sixties era. "I have to do these scenes and I'm meeting Nick Carter and Michelle Branch and I'm so nervous. It's kind of freaky," Brittany confesses, noting that her real life sometimes parallels her TV persona. "Meg is living out her dream being on *American Bandstand* and I'm living out my dreams being on *American Dreams*. I have to say these lines like, 'I'm having the best time of my life, and I don't want it to end.' And I thought, 'Wait a minute, I *am* having the best time of my life and I don't want it to end.'"

FILL-IN FAVES:

Brittany is all smiles—she's living out her wildest dreams.

Brittany likes ice cream with cookie flavors. If I could invent my own flavor of ice cream it would contain the following ingredients: _____.

*American Dreams* features pop music from the 1960s. I like to listen to

    a) rap music.

    b) pop music.

    c) my father sing in the shower.

If I could live in another era, I would chose a) the 1960s; b) the 1950s; c) the 1980s because _____.

# KristinKreuk

| | |
|---|---|
| **BIRTHDATE:** | December 30, 1982 |
| **ASTRO SIGN:** | Capricorn |
| **HOMETOWN:** | Vancouver, British Columbia |
| **FIRST GIG:** | *Edgemont*, a Canadian television series |
| **BIG BREAK:** | Landing the lead role of Lana Lang in the Superman drama *Smallville* |
| **WHAT'S NEXT:** | The third season of *Smallville* |
| **FAVORITE LIP GLOSS:** | DuWop Lip Venom |
| **HOBBIES:** | Reading, swimming, dancing, writing |
| **FAVE BOOKS:** | *Wuthering Heights, Anne of Green Gables,* and *Little Women.* |
| **WHAT SHE WATCHES:** | *Friends, ER, Third Watch* |
| **FAVE ACTRESS:** | Jodie Foster |

It's pretty great to be Kristin Kreuk these days. She stars as wholesome Lana Lang on the hit WB series *Smallville* and gets to work every day with Tom Welling (a.k.a. Clark Kent) and Michael Rosenbaum (a.k.a. Lex Luthor) — two of the hottest guys on television. "Tom is beautiful," Kristin says. But if she had her choice she'd probably go for a Lex Luthor type. "Lex is just so interesting and always charming. But I don't think you'd want to stay with him long-term," she says.

At only twenty years of age, Kristin is one of Hollywood's brightest stars. It's ironic, considering that when Kristin was a senior in high school she didn't think she wanted to pursue an acting career. "I wasn't sure. I thought I could still go to school in the fall. I didn't know," Kristin says.

That's because Kristin, a straight-A student who loved to read and dance and compete in gymnastics, thought of her drama class as a hobby. One day during her senior year at Eric Hamber High School, Kristin followed the advice of her drama teacher and went on an audition for a small Canadian television series about high school teens called *Edgemont*. She got the part — and that was the beginning of a new life for Kristin. A year later, in 2000, Kristin landed the lead role of Snow White in a made-for-TV movie and then *Smallville*.

The best thing of all for Kristin? She didn't have to move far away from her family to pursue her new career. *Smallville* is filmed in her hometown of Vancouver, British Columbia.

When she's not working, Kristin enjoys swimming, dancing, reading books, going shopping with her friends, and trying out new makeup products. Her philosophy on the makeup front is "a little bit goes a long way." Mascara, blush, and a little lip gloss are the three things Kristin swears by.

The sky is the limit for Kristin in terms of her career. She may put things on hold for a while so she can go to college and study psychology or environmental studies (that was the plan before her career took off). In the meantime she's happy to be working on a hit like *Smallville*. Success, Kristin says, hasn't changed her. "I get recognized on the street now, which is strange, sometimes nice and flattering. I've got the same friends, I do the same things. I just have more money to spend now."

love this job. I am working with the most talented group of people." — Kristin

**FILL-IN FAVES:**

My favorite superhero is _____

because _____.

I enjoy reading _____.

If I could spend the afternoon with Kristin, I would invite her to

a) go shopping.

b) go to the movies.

c) get some frozen yogurt and go for a walk.

# Mary-Kate and Ashley Olsen

| | |
|---|---|
| **BIRTHDATE**: | June 13, 1986 (Ashley is two minutes older than Mary-Kate) |
| **ASTRO SIGN**: | Gemini |
| **HOMETOWN**: | Los Angeles, California |
| **FIRST GIG**: | The TV sitcom *Full House* |
| **WHAT'S NEXT**: | College, plus more CDs, videos, and feature films |
| **NICKNAMES**: | Ashley is Ash and Mary-Kate is M-K |
| **FAVORITE LIP GLOSS**: | Ashley likes Rosebud Salve and Chanel Sheer; Mary-Kate's choice is Cherry Chapstick |
| **FAVORITE SUBJECT**: | Ashley likes math and science; Mary-Kate prefers English |
| **HOBBIES**: | Ashley likes shopping, Pilates, and golf while Mary-Kate enjoys horseback riding and yoga |
| **ROLE MODELS**: | Oprah Winfrey, Drew Barrymore |

They were huge television stars before they even knew how to walk. At seventeen, they are more popular than anyone else in their age group. There probably isn't a soul on the planet who doesn't know about Mary-Kate and Ashley Olsen.

Beginning at the tender age of nine months, Mary-Kate and Ashley took turns starring as adorable wide-eyed witty tyke Michelle Tanner on the hit show *Full House*. The two were such a team (hey, they walked alike, talked alike) they started doing everything together. And why not? As twins they each had a built-in best friend in the other — not to mention double the wardrobe!

*Full House* was the show to watch then, and is still hugely popular today in reruns. The reason is simple: Mary-Kate and Ashley. The two decided to branch out from the show when they were six. They formed their own production company and put out a video, *Our First Video*, and a CD, *Brother for Sale*. Their young fans couldn't get enough, so the girls continued with more straight-to-video movies, CDs, and, later, books and video games. It was then the two decided they would no longer be one, so to speak. When *Full House* ended in 1995, the two continued to work together, but as two different characters. That way Mary-Kate and Ashley would each get to show their individuality. But being a twin does have its advantages. "Sometimes when we look at each other, we know what the other's thinking," Ashley says.

Their true personalities soon emerged as they filmed more than two dozen video movies, like *When in Rome* and *The Adventures of Mary-Kate and Ashley*, plus the television series *Two of a Kind*. Ashley is the quiet and shy one while Mary-Kate is more outgoing and sporty. When it comes to fashion, for example, Ashley prefers frilly, more feminine styles while Mary-Kate favors

Who's who? (left to right: Mary-Kate; Ashley)

"Sometimes when we look at each other, we know what the other's thinking" —Ashley

funky, sporty duds. They recently launched a totally cool clothing line at Wal-Mart. "Ashley is probably a little more sophisticated," Mary-Kate admits. "Maybe I'd wear stripes and polka dots and she'd wear stripes with stripes. Ashley does the shopping for both of us. I don't usually shop a lot."

They also have different tastes in guys. Like, are they more into Justin Timberlake or Jack Osborne? Both are diplomatic. "Justin for his looks and Jack for his humor," Ashley says. And Mary-Kate? "Oh my gosh! Justin. I don't think I'm quite on Jack's level," she says.

What's true is that there are few who are on Mary-Kate and Ashley's level. They balance career and schoolwork and still have time for their friends and their fans. These gals tend to be modest when it comes to their undeniable talent and charm. But Hollywood isn't shy about noticing them. Drew Barrymore invited them to be a part of the blockbuster film *Charlie's Angels: Full Throttle*. *People* magazine named them two of their 50 Most Beautiful People. And in 2004, the dynamic duo will be honored with a star on the prestigious Hollywood Walk of Fame. That's great, Ashley says. But first things first. "S.A.T.'s and college."

Mary-Kate and Ashley are best friends.
My best friend is __Emily__ and together we like to __shop__.

Ashley thinks clothes are so much fun to shop for. My favorite store is
__Limited too.__

Ashley and Mary-Kate look alike, but they are very different. Ashley is more shy
and reserved than Mary-Kate. I'm more like _____.

# SolangeKnowles

| | |
|---|---|
| BIRTHDATE: | June 24, 1986 |
| ASTRO SIGN: | Cancer |
| HOMETOWN: | Houston, Texas |
| FIRST GIG: | Background dancer for Destiny's Child |
| WHAT'S NEXT: | The movie *Johnson Family Vacation* with Vanessa L. Williams, Bow Wow, and Cedric the Entertainer |
| FAVORITE SNACK FOOD: | Cheetos |
| PETS: | A Chihuahua named Shuggie |
| ACTING MENTOR: | Vanessa L. Williams |
| FAVORITE LIP GLOSS: | Lip D'Votion |
| HOBBIES: | Shopping, talking on the phone, writing music |

What do you do when your sister is the lead singer of one of the hottest all-girl groups in the world? If you're Solange Knowles, you watch, learn, and then go out and do it yourself. Like her big sister, Beyoncé, Solange acts and sings and dances. Basically, she does everything. And why not? "I'm an entertainer," Solange declares.

Solange is only seventeen, but already she's proved that she is not "Beyoncé Jr." No, Solange is a star in her own right. She even named her first album *Solo Star* as a way to emphasize that she doesn't live in her sister's shadow at all. "This record is a representation of my life," Solange says. "It's a real sense of who I am right now, and how I feel."

She was only four years old when she declared to her family that she wanted to be a performer for a living. Solange took singing lessons and performed with a children's dance troupe.

Because her dad, Matthew, is an entertainment manager, he had a little pull with local venues. Solange explains, "Anywhere my sisters [she considers all of the members of Destiny's Child her family] were singing, my dad would try and get me on the bill as well. I'd open up for them even when they were opening up for someone else." It was cool to sing in front of appreciative audiences, and Solange didn't disappoint.

She got her big break in 1999 when Destiny's Child was on tour. One of the group's dancers had to leave the tour at the last minute. There was no time to audition and train a replacement dancer. Luckily there was no need to. Solange had seen the group rehearse so many times, she knew the dance moves by heart. She jumped right in and didn't miss a beat. It still impresses her big sis to this day. "Her dance moves are incredible. I can't believe that's my little sister on stage," Beyoncé says.

She's been busy on her feet ever since. These days, Solange spends much of her time writing and producing music. She cowrote and produced many of the songs on her own album, and even helped out Destiny's Child singer Kelly Rowland with her solo album. In her free time she kicks around town with her Chihuahua, Shuggie, and close pal Bow Wow.

It's a family affair as Solange lends supports to big sis Beyoncé at the *Austin Powers 2* premiere. *(left to right: dad: Matthew Knowles; Beyoncé; Solange; mom: Tina Knowles)*

"I'm not just a teen singer," Solange says. "I really put a lot of myself in my music. I really think it's important that young people do for themselves and not allow anyone to shape them or create them."

**FILL-IN FAVES:**

Solange likes wearing funky-colored sneakers with her outfits. My favorite article of clothing is _____ because _____.

Solange has experienced so many neat things by getting to travel and dance and perform all over the country. If I could ask Solange one thing it would be this: would you like to be a cheer leader with me?

Solange admires Vanessa L. Williams. The person I admire most is _____ _____ because _____.

# HilaryDuff

| | |
|---|---|
| BIRTHDATE: | September 28, 1987 |
| ASTRO SIGN: | Libra |
| HOMETOWN: | Houston, Texas |
| FIRST GIG: | *True Women*, a 1997 television miniseries that starred Angelina Jolie |
| BIG BREAK: | The title role in the Disney Channel's *Lizzie McGuire* |
| WHAT'S NEXT: | Two feature films, *Cheaper by the Dozen* and *A Cinderella Story*; WB music special *Hilary Duff's Birthday Celebration* and a new solo CD |
| NICKNAME: | Hil |
| PETS: | Two dogs, Lil Dog and Remington |
| FAVORITE FOODS: | Okra and olives |
| FAVORITE SUBJECT: | History |
| FAVORITE LIP GLOSS: | MAC Lip Glass and Stila Lip Shines |
| ACTING ROLE MODELS: | Sandra Bullock and Cameron Diaz |
| HOBBIES: | Music, shopping, in-line skating, swimming |

**Y**ou can't get enough of Hilary Duff these days. The *Lizzie McGuire* star has been everywhere. Not only does she have a cool television show, but she scored big time this year with back-to-back films *Agent Cody Banks* and *The Lizzie McGuire Movie*. Hilary also sings her show's theme song and is working on a new solo CD. As if that's not enough, she's got two more movies in the works for 2004 — *Cheaper by the Dozen* and *The Cinderella Story*. Oh, and then there's a Hilary clothing line in the works, too.

Hilary with her cartoon alter-ego on *Lizzie McGuire*.

At sixteen, she's definitely way busier than most teenagers, but that's how Hilary likes it. "I'm pretty young, so I don't think of it as work," she says, noting that there are times "I won't even know what I'm doing the next day, and I'll just have to go do it and be told right before I run on. But I love that."

When Hilary was a young girl growing up in Houston she enjoyed ballet dancing and traveled with the BalletMet Columbus production of *The Nutcracker*. In 1997, Hilary got her first professional acting gig in the TV miniseries *True Women*. She was officially bitten by the acting bug. She landed two more roles in TV movies, *Casper Meets Wendy* and *The Soul Collector*. Then, in 2000, Hilary was cast in the sitcom *Daddio*. But after shooting the first episode the producers felt she wasn't quite right for the part after all. Hilary was crushed! "I was, like, wanting to quit," she says, "and I had one audition left, and it was *Lizzie McGuire*."

Thank goodness she hung in there! Lizzie couldn't be a better match for Hilary, who sometimes finds herself in the same situations she encounters on the show. "Girls are just trying to find out who they are at this stage, and that's totally what Lizzie is about," Hilary says.

Last spring Hilary starred as Frankie Muniz's girlfriend in *Agent Cody Banks*. In real life, Hilary says she and Frankie are "just friends." But that's not to say she doesn't have a crush or two . . . or three. "Oh, so many boys, so little time," she jokes. Her current faves are Brad Pitt, Justin Timberlake, and Shane West. And she's also been known to hang out with Aaron Carter.

Sure, she wears cool clothes and gets to meet hot guys. But when you get down to it, Hilary is like any normal teenager. She likes to hang with her friends at the mall and sleep in on Saturdays.

"I think I live a pretty typical life," says Hilary. "I have to clean my room and do chores on the weekends. I have homework, and sometimes I fight with my sister. I think I'm pretty normal," she says.

When things get hectic, Hilary sometimes wonders what it's like to go to a normal high school and not be recognized everywhere you go. But those thoughts are fleeting. "Mom and Dad keep asking, 'Are you sure you don't want to go back to Texas and be a normal teenager?' I'm like, 'No!'" Hilary says, "I have bad days, like everyone else, but I keep them in perspective and just wait for the sun to shine again."

Hilary hangs with singing superstar Aaron Carter.

FILL-IN FAVES:

Nicknames are cool. Hilary's friends call her Hil. My friends call me
_____ Sydster _____.

If Hilary came to my hometown, I'd show her around and we could do
_____ together.

Hilary's favorite subject is history. My favorite history topic is
_____ because _____.

# Breakout Alert!

## Kaley Cuoco

Good things are in the works for these four up-and-comers . . . .

### KALEY'S KWIK HITS

| | |
|---|---|
| **BIRTHDATE:** | November 30, 1985 |
| **ASTRO SIGN:** | Sagittarius |
| **HOMETOWN:** | Thousand Oaks, California |
| **FIRST GIG:** | A small role in the 1992 TV movie *Quicksand: No Escape* |
| **WHAT'S NEXT:** | The second season of *8 Simple Rules for Dating My Teenage Daughter*, the movie *The Hollow* with Backstreet Boy Nick Carter (it's a present-day version of the horror classic *The Legend of Sleepy Hollow*). |
| **FAVORITE LIP GLOSS:** | Rosebud Salve |
| **SNACKS ON:** | Red rope licorice |
| **LOVES TO WEAR:** | Seven jeans |
| **HOBBIES:** | Tennis, shopping |

Kaley Cuoco's future is looking very bright, thanks to her star turn as John Ritter's boy-crazy, spree-shopping daughter on the hit ABC show *8 Simple Rules for Dating My Teenage Daughter*. Cutie Kaley began modeling and doing local commercials when she was six years old. Then she landed a series of acting gigs in feature films like *Virtuosity* and *Picture Perfect* and in television shows like *My So-Called Life, Ellen, 7th Heaven*, and *Growing Up Brady*. Kaley is also a tennis freak. In fact, she was a nationally ranked player at age fourteen. "I traveled all around and was pretty good," she says. Look for Kaley in 2004 when she stars with Nick Carter in the big screen thriller *The Hollow*.

### FILL-IN FAVES:

Kaley likes to play tennis. My favorite sport is ___Cheerleading___.

Kaley likes to snack on red rope licorice. When I feel like snacking I grab _____.

# Emily Van Camp

BIRTHDATE: May 12, 1986
ASTRO SIGN: Taurus
HOMETOWN: Port Perry, Ontario
FIRST GIG: At age twelve Emily appeared in a local grocery store commercial where she skated on a giant pot of ice cream
WHAT'S NEXT: The second season of *Everwood*; the movie *A Different Loyalty* with Sharon Stone
FAVORITE LIP GLOSS: Kiehl's or MAC Lip Glass
HOBBIES: Dancing, hiking, photography, yoga
FAVORITE ACTRESS: Audrey Hepburn
LIKES TO EAT: Popsicles

Dancing is Emily Van Camp's first love, but years ago when she visited her older sister (also a dancer) on a Montreal movie set, she found a new passion — acting. It didn't take long for the seventeen-year-old to make it big. She stars on the WB's *Everwood*, where she plays Amy Nicole Abbott, a high school beauty who befriends Ephram (Gregory Smith), the brooding new guy in town. Not coincidentally, Amy's a ballet dancer, too!

Shy Emily is a natural talent who found an agent and landed her first television commercial at age twelve. A year later she was cast in the TV miniseries *Jackie O: A Life Story*. At fifteen, she starred in the short-lived TV series *Glory Days* with Eddie Cahill. Then *Everwood* came along. Next up for Emily is finishing high school, of course, and a role in the upcoming Sharon Stone feature film *A Different Loyalty*. She still enjoys dancing. But, Emily says, "When I'm working, I feel like I was totally destined to act — as corny as that sounds."

## FILL-IN FAVES:

When Emily wants some time to herself she goes hiking. I enjoy doing
___dancing___ by myself.

Emily is originally from Canada, but travels to the United States to work. My favorite place to travel is _____.

# JenniferFreeman

| | |
|---|---|
| **BIRTHDATE:** | October 20, 1985 |
| **ASTRO SIGN:** | Libra |
| **HOMETOWN:** | Long Beach, California |
| **BIG BREAK:** | A guest-starring role on *7th Heaven* |
| **WHAT'S NEXT:** | The fourth season of *My Wife and Kids*; *Johnson Family Vacation* with Vanessa L. Williams, Cedric the Entertainer, and Bow Wow; *You Got Served* with B2K; Neutrogena ad campaign beginning in winter 2004 |
| **WHAT SHE WATCHES:** | *Buffy the Vampire Slayer* |
| **HOBBIES:** | Writing, singing, swimming, playing basketball, and shopping |
| **WHO SHE ADMIRES:** | Julia Stiles and Natalie Portman, because they haven't let their careers interfere with pursuing a college education |
| **FAVE SUBJECT:** | English |

When Jennifer Freeman was nine years old, a talent manager spotted her in a grocery store and thought she would make an excellent model and actress. "She gave my mother a card and ever since I've been acting," says Jennifer, who stars as teenager Claire Kyle on ABC's *My Wife and Kids*.

Jennifer's career began with modeling and commercial work. She then landed a series of guest-starring roles on shows like *Even Stevens*, *Lizzie McGuire*, and *7th Heaven*. She also performed in Los Angeles-area productions of *The Wiz* and *The Gift*. Next year film fans can catch Jennifer in the comedy *Johnson Family Vacation*, with Cedric the Entertainer, Vanessa L. Williams, and Bow Wow. She will also star with B2K in the feature *You Got Served*.

## FILL-IN FAVES:

Jennifer's astrological sign is Libra. I was born on _____ and my astrological sign is _____.

If I could spend the day with Jennifer, I would invite her to _Shoping_.

# AlexaVega

BIRTHDATE: August 27, 1988
ASTRO SIGN: Virgo
HOMETOWN: Miami, Florida
FIRST GIG: The television series *Evening Shade* — she played Burt Reynolds's daughter
BIG BREAK: *Spy Kids* with Antonio Banderas and Carla Gugino
WHAT'S NEXT: *Spy Kids 3-D: Game Over*
FAVORITE LIP GLOSS: Bonne Bell Cotton Candy Lipsmacker
HOBBIES: Dancing, reading, gymnastics
FAVE SUBJECT: Math

It's no mystery why Alexa Vega is successful. On her first job, at the young age of five, she wowed Burt Reynolds when she played his daughter on the television series *Evening Shade*. Ever since, Alexa has been wowing Hollywood with pivotal roles in movies like *Twister* (she played a young Helen Hunt), *Ghosts of Mississippi* (she starred as Alec Baldwin's daughter), and *The Deep End of the Ocean* (she played Michelle Pfeiffer's daughter). Her breakthrough came when she landed the role of Carmen Cortez, a young female James Bond, if you will, in the popular *Spy Kids* movie trilogy. Many fans admire Alexa, which makes the high school sophomore a little uneasy. "It's kind of weird and exciting that someone looks up to you so much," she confesses. In the end, she says, "I'm just a normal kid."

## FILL-IN FAVES:

Alexa gets to use some really cool gadgets in the *Spy Kids* movies. I wish I had a gadget that could __do my home work__.

Math is Alexa's favorite subject in school. My favorite subject is _____ because _____.

# TAKE THE TEEN QUEEN QUIZ!

So just how well do you think you know your fave teen stars? Here's a little quiz to test your knowledge. The answers are at the bottom of the page. But remember, NO PEEKING!!!

1) Amanda Bynes made her acting debut on what Nickelodeon show?
   a) *None of This*
   b) *All That*
   c) *Everybody Loves Hamburgers*
   d) *Got Milk?*

2) Which of the Olsen twins is older, and by how much?
   a) Ashley, by two minutes
   b) Ashley, by four hours
   c) Mary-Kate, by two weeks

3) People have been raving about this former *Cosby Show* star since she was three years old.
   a) Britney Spears
   b) Raven
   c) Nelly Furtado

4) She used to be an ace on the court, but this gal followed a few simple rules and became a TV star instead.
   a) Melissa Joan Hart
   b) Venus Williams
   c) Kaley Cuoco

5) When this beauty's wig fell off during a performance of the musical *Pirates of Penzance*, it was an American dream of the embarrassing kind!
   a) Britney Spears
   b) Beyoncé Knowles
   c) Brittany Snow

6) She became an overnight success when a FedEx deliveryman referred her to a record executive. He believed she was *more* than just a pretty face, and so do we!
   a) Mandy Moore
   b) Pink
   c) Madonna

7) This down-to-earth gal likes to keep *busy*, and never lets her hectic schedule get her in a *tizzy*.
   a) Hilary Duff
   b) Oprah Winfrey
   c) Angelina Jolie

8) She danced her way to fame with Destiny's Child and said "so long" to anonymity.
   a) Amanda Bynes
   b) Kelly Clarkson
   c) Solange Knowles

9) This fresh-faced beauty hit the big time when her *small*-town TV show premiered two years ago to *super* reviews.
   a) Kristin Kreuk
   b) Tori Spelling
   c) Jenna Elfman

10) She finds *everlasting* peace every time she shops at Target.
   a) Katie Couric
   b) Barbara Walters
   c) Alexis Bledel